A LifeWay Ministry

TRUE LOVE WAITS

Takes a Look at
Courting, Dating, & Hanging Out

The Girls' Book

David Payne
With Raymond and Hannah Vogtner,
Kristi Cherry, Tracey Bumpus,
and Matt Tullos

LifeWay Press®
Nashville, Tennessee

ISBN: 978-0-6330-0463-7

Item 001114514

Dewey Decimal Classification Number: 306.73

Subject Heading: TEENAGERS / SEXUAL BEHAVIOR / DATING / SOCIAL CUSTOMS

Printed in the United States of America

Student Ministry Publishing
LifeWay Church Resources
One LifeWay Plaza
Nashville, TN 37234-0144

We believe that the Bible has God for its author; salvation for its end; and truth, without any
mixture of error, for its matter and that all Scripture is totally true and trustworthy.
The 2000 statement of *The Baptist Faith and Message* is our doctrinal guideline.

Unless otherwise indicated, Scripture quotations are from
the Holy Bible, New International Version. Copyright © 1973, 1978, 1984
by International Bible Society. Used by permission.

Contents

You Go Girl!

Being a Real Woman

Laura looked at the magazine rack in a shop in Chicago's airport. The more she looked, the more depressed she became. Cover after cover she found herself confronted by the images of thin, perfectly sculpted bodies. She thought to herself, "How am I supposed to be a success if I have to compete with these girls?"

Her eyes scanned the titles of the articles, "Making Your Man Scream with Delight," "Romance Tricks That Really Work," "I lost 25 pounds and gained a husband who plays for the Chargers."

She couldn't help wondering what it would take for her to find someone or something to make her life a success. As she walked through the airport terminal she caught a glimpse of herself in a mirror mounted on the wall. She moved quickly out of view and tried to erase the image from her mind. *I hate myself,* she thought.

Obviously Laura has a problem; and if she doesn't stop the voice of pessimism in her life, she'll grow depressed. She might even try to reach for a pain killer. Society and media have squeezed her into their mold, and now she feels like a wounded animal trapped by unrealistic expectations.

What messages do the world's culture, media, art, and society transmit about the meaning of a woman?_____

_____

_____

_____

_____

In three sentences, write your definition of femininity.

_____

_____

_____

What Does It Mean to Be a Woman?

Women through the ages have been known for the ability to sway the thoughts and hearts of men. Some girls do this through an engaging smile. Some do it through the creative use of makeup. Some girls rely on low-cut dresses and a well-timed wink.

What kind of message do you send out to guys? Is it one of strength and self-confidence or one of desperation and loneliness? Are you relying on your personality to speak for you, or is your appearance doing all the talking? Be careful about the influence you have over the opposite sex. Your femininity is a gift from God. It should be used only according to His purposes.

The Hormone Factor

How can you be a woman when you are still just a teenager? The answer to that question is that physically and anatomically, you are no different than a woman who is in college. The real differences are in the amount of experience that someone with more years has and in the amount of hormones released into the young body.

Hormonal changes start when you are very young and explode in the early teen years. Hormones, in a very sneaky and insidious way, are slowly released into your body, causing differences in the way your body works and in the way your mind thinks. Once these hormones start spilling over into your body, it is something that will happen for the rest of your life. As this continues, you will have to deal with your hormones in an appropriate way.

Read *1 Corinthians 6:19*. The instruction given here is to honor God with your body. This is a blanket statement with no exceptions. It does not say honor God with your body except when your hormones are raging. How can you honor God with your body? List all the possible ways here (not just sexual ones). _____

_____

_____

_____

_____

So, What Is a Woman?

Women are emotional creatures. They like to feel loved and taken care of. One way they can receive this is in a physical relationship. A physical, sexual relationship with a man provides the physical contact they crave and a perceived emotional connection. However, be forewarned that this emotional connection is a sham. Guys do not go into a physical relationship for the same reasons girls do. Guys generally are simply satisfying a hormonal urge. Once this has been satisfied, they no longer are interested in the other person.

God does not want His daughters to be used in this way. He wants us to be secure enough in who we are in Him to wait until the right man comes along. Only within the context of marriage are we to then give ourselves physically. What a woman has to learn is to allow God to mature her to where her identity is not wrapped up in what

6

other people think of her, but in what God thinks of her. A woman is what God created you to be. Seek to be obedient to His commands and to grow in your relationship with Him, and you will become a godly woman.

Who We Are in Christ

Do You Really Like Yourself?
Do you like yourself the way you are? Do you feel good about yourself? Is there anything about you, you wish you could change?

If you are dissatisfied with who you are, you are not alone. Most young people do not like something about themselves. It could be their appearance, their personality, their size, their voice, or their nose. Oftentimes these feelings of dissatisfaction can cause us to withdraw and become antisocial. This is a bad move.

Before we can love others, we must first love ourselves. In *Ephesians 5:28*, Paul says that husbands should love their wives as their own bodies. The assumption here being that before a man can really love his wife, he has to first have a good feeling about himself and his own body. The same holds true for women. Before a woman can truly love her husband, she has to first love herself.

Who Does Like You?
At times, we all feel unloved and useless. It is not our feelings or our usefulness that determine our lovability. What determines it is how God feels about us. The Bible teaches that we are made in the image of God. The Bible also teaches that God is like a loving Father to us. He loves us and cares for us. If you ever doubt your worth to God, consider the price He paid for you and your forgiveness through His Son, Jesus Christ.

Alike But Different

One look at your younger brother or a glance in the mirror will tell you that you, as a female, are different from the male species. Duh! It is truly an obvious statement, but when males interact with females and females interact with males, in some ways they expect the other gender to think the same way as they do. So, the obvious reminder remains. You *are* different!

The physical differences are obvious. But males and females are also alike. They are both created in the image of God (*Gen. 1:27*), and their basic physical forms are somewhat similar. The social differences, however, are more pronounced.

When girls talk, what do they most often talk about? List as many different topics as you can think of. _____

_____

_____

_____

How We Are Wired

Don't feel like you are a horrible person if you think about sex. However, a preoccupation with sex and the guys you are around may lead you into compromise. Constantly entertaining these thoughts will eventually cause you to give in when Satan presents you the opportunity. Here are a few tips if you feel that you are struggling with power over your sex drive:

1. Find two or three other girls and develop an accountability agreement. Meet and pray together that you will all remain true to your Christian values. Take the first step to start this support group. I'm sure that the other girls will be glad you did!

2. Don't feed the fire with sexually explicit fuel: MTV, teen mags, romance novels, other forms of trash media. Don't trust yourself with unfiltered internet access. (Check out *www.lifewayonline.com*)

3. Don't buy into the lie that long, deep kissing is part of the romantic scene and won't lead to something more. It does not work that way. Chances are, you or the guy you're with will end up wanting more, and you'll wind up compromising your values (and his). After this you experience a flood of guilt, the likes of which you have never experienced. It's not fulfilling and you could permanently corrupt your sexual identity and self-image.

4. Don't condemn yourself for having a sex drive. Sex is a beautiful gift that is reserved for marriage. Unfortunately, you received the drive to express that gift several years before you would normally marry. So avoid the traps mentioned earlier and don't spend time raking yourself through the coals about having passing thoughts about sex.

List any other ideas that have worked for you in your attempt to preserve your womanhood and sexual purity.

_____

_____

_____

_____

_____

Top 10 Lies & Cop-outs
Avoiding Head-on Collisions

After an extensive survey of students, youth pastors, parents, teachers, and hot dog vendors, we proudly present: The Top Ten Lies and Cop-outs of Courting and Dating—from the home office in Sioux City, Iowa.

The List

10. My relationships will be just like those I see on TV and in the movies.

This lie appeals to our romantic nature and our desire to be loved. If you believed relationships worked like those you see on TV and movies, you might find yourself spending half of your life in a coffee shop waiting for the guy who lives across the hall from you to come and sweep you off your feet, or you could leave three men at the altar because you haven't found Richard Gere yet.

The happily-ever-after theme is constant on TV and in Hollywood and is even taught to us at a very early age in our bedtime stories. Sure, someday you will probably meet your knight in shining armor; but that doesn't mean that every day with him you will feel like a queen.

Reality is that relationships are hard work. At the end of a 30-minute segment, all of your problems won't be solved.

Soap operas and romance novels are traps for young women. Such fantasy can easily fill your mind and become your expectations. In case you haven't been out in the social circle lately, there aren't too many beautiful guys out there whose dad has given them the family business at which they never have to work so they have time to plan a romantic picnic in the woods where they will feed you strawberries and give you a diamond necklace for no reason! What's even better is that there are guys out there who love the Lord, will love to get to know the real you, will be true to you, and treat you better than a queen!

9. He told me he loves me, so that means he respects me.

Many girls get hurt by believing this lie. It is easy for a guy to say he loves you, but it is harder for him to mean it. A guy knows that a girl desires to be loved by someone. He also thinks that if he tells you he loves you, then you will be like putty in his hands. A guy who respects you will not pressure you to compromise your standards and will not degrade you.

You have to be very cautious when a guy says those three little words. Along with love should come actions that show love. *First Corinthians 13* tells us what love is. If his actions don't comply with this Scripture, you should beware of his motives. When he says he loves you and he means it, then it should also mean he respects you; and his actions will reflect that.

8. If I have sex with him, our relationship will improve.

If you are being pressured to have sex with him and are experiencing problems in the relationship, the tendency may be to give in and have sex with him. You may think that the other problems will go away.

Well, they probably will—for one night! The next day, the relationship will be just the same, if not worse. You will realize then that sex did not solve the problems between the two of you. Now, every intimate detail of your body, your senses, and your mind are stripped away. Every boundary is torn down, and the experience cannot be erased from your mind.

7. The skimpy clothes I wear have nothing to do with the way guys act around me.

Males are easily aroused by sight. And I do mean easily! *Romans 14:13* instructs us to *"make up your mind not to put any stumbling block or obstacle in your brother's way."* If seeing you in a tight shirt, which shows all of the curves God gave you, triggers a guy's fantasy mode to kick in and causes him to lust, then you are being a stumbling block.

You say it's not your fault that God made males that way! Correct. But you do have the responsibility to be an encourager, not an obstacle in his path to righteousness.

So how are you to know if he is lusting because of your attire? _____

_____

_____

Well, you can pretty much be sure that if there is no extra space between your skin and your shirt, then he is probably getting too much information.

Your clothes say a lot about you. Most teens would say they express themselves with what they wear. Do you want to express yourself as a sexy, let-it-all-hang-out stumbling block, or a respectable, God-honoring young woman? _____

_____

Do you need to reconsider your wardrobe? Do you need to start honoring God with your attire? _____

_____

_____

6. Everybody's having sex.

I don't know who started this rumor, but it sure has gotten around. Maybe every character on TV is having sex and maybe every person in those music videos is having sex, but less than 50 percent of real-life teens are doing it.[1]

5. Any sexual act is OK as long as I don't have intercourse.

This lie is becoming more and more accepted due to the deteriorating morality of society. God calls us to be pure, which sure is different from what the world calls us to be.

Fill in the blanks.

How can a young man _____ his way _____? By _____
according to _____ _____. Psalm 119:9

Don't let anyone _____ _____ on you because _____
_____ _____, but set an _____ for the believers in
speech, in life, in love, in faith and in _____. I Timothy 4:12

Blessed are the _____ ____ _____, for they will see God.
Matthew 5:8

It is God's will that you should be _____: that you should
avoid sexual _____; that each of you should learn to
_____ his own _____ in a way that is _____ and
_____, not in passionate _____ like the heathen, who
do not _____ God; I Thessalonians 4:3-5

Put _____ _____, therefore, _____ belongs to your earthly nature: _____ immorality, _____, _____...
Colossians 3:5

4. If I don't get practice with relationships now, I will never be a good wife.

Practice doesn't make perfect when it comes to marriage, sex, and romance. In fact, practice does just the opposite. Constantly being involved in serious relationships before the ring slips on the finger only cheapens the future. It makes what God intended to be extraordinary very commonplace. The only thing you'll need to practice before you marry is saying that powerful two letter word—"NO." Saying "no" now making saying "yes" at the altar incredibly exhilarating. So your choice is this:

Act married, say "I love you," make phony commitments before you're married and when you find the right man to marry, regret that you didn't save the treasures of love for him alone.
OR
Make a commitment to treat your personality, sexuality, words, and lifestyle as a sacred treasure reserved for one man and one pure destiny.

3. I owe my date something for taking me out.

This relates back to the whole respect thing. A date who respects you will never make you believe this lie. In fact, this lie infers what is known as prostitution.

2. We will probably get married someday, so being intimate with him now won't hurt anything.

Girls in serious relationships at an early age (high school) will be most vulnerable to this lie. In reality, very few high school sweethearts stay together after graduation. Many youthful years await you after high school, during which you may move away from home, find a new group of friends, change some interests, and become the young woman God wants you to become. Don't rush. Save yourself.

1. I need to be in a relationship to be complete.

The only relationship that you need in order to be complete is your relationship with Jesus. You can find your satisfaction and your contentment in Him. No human can fill that void; it's a God-shaped hole. He created us that way.

Did you ever wonder why, after trying so many times to feel complete by having a boyfriend, you still had that empty, unfulfilled spot in your heart? _____

_____

_____

Commit today to start filling that void with Jesus and not with relationships with guys. Pray that He come and make you complete. Let Him be your all.

I know what it is to be in need, and I know what it is to have plenty. I have learned to secret of being content in any and every situation, whether well fed or hungry, whether living in plenty or in want. I can do everything through him who gives me strength. Philippians 4:12-13

_____

1. "The Naked Truth," *Newsweek*, 8 May 2000, p. 58.

15

Getting Started in Dating or Courting

Getting Your Signals Straight

In this session we'll take a look at the definitions of dating and courting and also how both of these strategies begin. As you read the material and work through these issues, begin to pray that God will give you courage and an open mind to choose courting, dating, or hanging out. Let's go!

Is dating just a social outing? A casual acquaintance? What is it? It would be very easy to quickly adopt a bad definition of dating. What is your definition of dating? _____

_____

_____

_____

Which one of the following opinions sounds most like you?

❑ Dating is such a sham! It's all so fake. Once you go out with a guy, it's like he freaks out and thinks you're trying to get all emotionally attached. Gag! Who needs that?

❑ Dating is fun. I love the way it makes me feel when I'm getting to know a guy. First kisses are the best. I don't like to lead guys on; but I do enjoy flirting, if you know what I mean. So do I think about dating as a prelude to marriage? Not really.

❏ I can tell you this. Dating is another word for time bomb. It will end up in just a ton of hurt feelings and moral compromise. I want to find a mate in the next 10 years, but dating is not the way I want to find him. I know that God will show me who I should marry. Until then, don't ask. I'll just say no.

So you don't like any of those? Write your own._____

_____

_____

_____

Let's think about the following statements. Do they ring true? Answer yes or no.

1. Dating almost always ends up in heartbreak. _____
2. Dating is a good way to lose your standards and maybe even your virginity. _____
3. Most of my friends date just to have fun. No one takes it seriously. It's just a warm-up for the day when we'll really be looking for a mate. _____

The Dating Destination

As you start dating, there are many challenges along the way. Before you ever begin dating someone, it is important to ask: Where is this relationship heading? If we continue to date, what is the destination? As females are generally more emotional than males, it is important that you have a destination in mind before you become entangled in the romance that so often accompanies dating. Start thinking this direction by answering the following question.

What is the goal of a dating relationship? _____

_____

_____

_____

For many, the goals are to have fun, to socialize, and to try and find the right person to marry.

The Dating Treasure Map!

Use the space below to draw a sort of treasure map. Start where you think you are right now and draw a map that includes the destinations you would like to visit during your dating life. Include destinations such as friendship, laughter, honest sharing, serving, intimacy, etc. Map out the path you would like your dating relationships to take.

The Dating Alternative

Jason and Katie had an interesting relationship. Their friends just couldn't quite figure it out. They did a lot of things together, but it always seemed to be with large groups of people or with their parents. No one ever recalled seeing them together alone, but all were under the impression that they were "exclusive." They had other friends who spent time together; and their relationships were hard to figure out, but it just seemed that they liked to hang out together. Something was different about Jason and Katie, however. Finally, one of their friends grew curious enough to ask Katie about their relationship, and she told them that they were courting. Her friend acted like she knew what she was talking about but really had no clue.

So What's Courtship?
Let's get a dictionary definition first and then work from there. *Webster's Ninth* defines the act of courting as, "to seek to gain or achieve, to seek the affections of, to seek to win a pledge of marriage from, to engage in social activities leading to engagement and marriage."[1]

Courtship is about open and honest exploration of each other's lives and families leading up to engagement and marriage. Courtship is about marriage—you court in order to see if you can be good friends with the person and to see if this is the person you can make a marriage commitment to. There is no romantic interaction until after the commitment to marriage.

Some parents and teens have become disappointed with the dating scene and the pain associated with feeling used in a relationship without commitment. An alternative is gaining popularity among some families. It's actually been around long before Romeo and Juliet were sneaking around trying to get a priest to marry them secretly.

Courtship is almost as old as the Bible! So what is courtship? Circle the best answer.
A. Finding a mate through a rigorous test of skills in the areas of Ping-Pong, ski boarding, and sailing.
B. Laws preventing mutiny of seafaring vessels.

19

C. A valid alternative to dating that avoids many of the traps, snags, and heartaches that are hard to avoid in the dating process.

If you chose C, you're on the right track. If you didn't, you may have fallen asleep as you were reading and had one of those weird pizza dreams. Before we dive into all this, let's clear up a few misconceptions.

Courtship is becoming more and more mainstream. You don't have to be a member of some strange religious sect. People who court rarely end up wearing a black Amish hat with a long beard (good news, ladies!). Also, courtship doesn't mean you must marry the person you begin courting. Courtship is a process of strong integrity, which says, "I take my future marriage seriously, and I won't open myself up to all the potential land mines I'm seeing in the dating process."

So What Is Courtship (REALLY)?

Here's a short description of the courtship model:

Boy meets girl. That's the way dating starts as well. But it will get different fast. (As in the next step...)

Instead of boy calls girl or girl calls boy, boy calls girl's parents. (Whoa! What a wild concept!) He sets up a meeting with the girl's parents to introduce himself to them while expressing his interest in spending time with their daughter. After this initial meeting, the parents talk with their daughter about this guy, and they share any concerns or observations they have. After that, if all parties are in agreement, the family finds ways to get the two together in appropriate and supervised settings with the express purpose of getting to know each other better.

Describing Courtship
Write some descriptive phrases about courtship._____

_____

_____

_____

Not many people understand the whole idea of courtship. In fact, if you took the time to do some simple research you would find varying views on courtship.

To some it is a romantic relationship that your parents approve of and are heavily involved in. Some say you should never touch your partner in a courting relationship—no hand holding, no putting your arm around him (even if you are just stretching), and no kissing. Others say that all time spent together is done so in groups. The couple is never alone. Many times they are out with one or both of their parents. One of the hopes is that this would be the only romantic relationship a person has before marriage, though that may not happen in some instances.

Is Courtship for You?
In a nutshell, the emphasis in courtship is to develop a close friendship in order to get to know each other well enough to see if you want to spend the rest of your life with the person. Marriage is the eventual goal of courtship just as it is in dating. Still, courtship is a hard concept for some to consider.

Are you willing to consider courtship as a possible path toward marriage?_____

If not, what frightens you most about courtship?_____

_____

_____

_____

Use the space below to write down what it would take to get you to consider courtship as a viable option to dating and hanging out. _____

_____

_____

_____

_____

_____

A Girl's Start-up Checklist

(Clarification: This is for you to fill out only. It is not recommended that you have a guy fill this out about himself!)

❑ **The Heart Check:** What is his relationship with the Lord? Has he shared with you how he became a Christian? Does he share his faith with others? Is church just a social opportunity, or does he have a real passion for God?

❑ **The Sight Check:** Is your relationship based on how he looks at you or how you look at him? Is he attracted to you simply because you stimulate him visually? (Remember: Guys are very visually oriented.) Are you choosing the relationship simply on the basis of his physical attraction to you? Does he look at you through the eyes of respect, or does he look at you through the eyes of lust?

❑ **The Needs Check:** Do you want to date him because he needs you? Trying to fill a need is not a good place to start for a dating relationship. A lot of guys are willing to let a girl "mother" them. If you feel this might be the case, remember that it's a bad place to start a dating relationship.

❑ **Emotional Check:** Does he express his emotions in a healthy way? Does he lose his temper easily? Does he seem to allow his

22

emotions to control him? Is he moody? Does he know how to communicate his emotions? The secret to successful emotional well- being is being able to express emotions in a Christlike manner.

❏ **The Words Check:** What words or thoughts dominate his conversation? Does his conversation drift into gray areas when he's using humor? Does he speak the best of people, or does he use his words as weapons? Do his conversations take on a different tone when he's with the guys?

❏ **Home Check:** What kind of relationship does he have with his father and mother? If he has brothers or sisters, how does he treat them? You can tell a lot about how a guy will treat you by looking at how he treats his mother.

❏ **Money Check:** What emphasis does he place on money? Do new cars, jewelry, and brand name clothes easily impress him?

❏ **Preoccupation Check:** What preoccupies him? Does he spend a lot of time flexing his muscles in front of the mirror? What addictive behaviors does he have?

Remember: Dating or courting should never be seen as an attempt to change a person. It's just too emotionally expensive and risky.

Hangin' Out & Havin' Fun! A Really Cool Option...

For many teenagers, their relationship with the opposite sex defies definition. If a guy and a girl go and do something together, it could be as friends or as acquaintances and may have no romantic overtones to it at all. The only description that even comes close is that they hang out together. Is hanging out different than courting? Is it different than dating? In some ways they are different, and in some ways they are the same.

To start with just hanging out and end up involved in a committed romantic relationship is a long journey. When you reach the end, however, it seems to have snuck up on you. You suddenly find yourself romantically attracted to a good friend. It's strange but true; this really happens!

Here are the big three reasons to consider hanging out as a viable alternative to heavy-duty dating.
• When you are with a group of committed friends you are less likely to be drawn into sexual temptation.
• Hanging with friends takes the pressure off of you. You don't have to be Miss Social Butterfly for the whole evening.
• No strings attached. When you go out with a group you can get to know a guy without a ton of pressure.

What are some other benefits of hanging out? _____
_____
_____
_____

Beware!
If you're going to hang out with a group, make sure you hang around with the right group.

Many students make the mistake of hanging with a crowd of their peers who are minimally committed to purity at best. Then when Friday night rolls around, they go to a party or a dance and find out that the crowd that seemed to be students of integrity were simply saving up their wild streaks for the weekend.

"One of the worst experiences I had last year was when I met some guys and girls at church who also happened to go to my school. I enjoyed being around them. Granted, they weren't exactly spiritual leaders in the youth group, but they were really nice and part of the popular crowd. Plus, there was a guy I was really interested in who usually hung out with them. He asked if I wanted to go to a party with them. I figured this was my opportunity to really be part of the 'in' crowd, so I went. I had a great time until I started making some choices I never thought I'd make. Maybe it was the guy that I liked, or maybe it was just that I didn't want them to think I was a prude. For whatever reason, I ended up getting totally wasted for the first time in my life. I felt horrible the next morning. But even more than the physical drain, I felt like I had spiritually trashed everything I stood for as a committed Christian."

Harold Morris, a well-known Christian writer who spent years inside the South Carolina State Penitentiary, simply stated it this way. "The friends you hang out with in many cases determine the direction of your life."[2]

Believe it. Corrupt or ungodly companions who try to fit you into their mold are dangerously controlling.

---

1. *Webster's Collegiate Dictionary,* 9th ed., s.v. "courtship."
2. Harold Morris, *Twice Pardoned* (Arcadia, California: Focus on the Family, 1986).

Session 4

Guidelines & Pitfalls

Getting Your Mind in Gear

I n this chapter we'll discuss some things that will be crucial if you choose to be righteous while courting, dating, or just hanging out.

Finding the right person– Being the right person

In today's society, many people are more focused on finding the right person than on being the right person God wants them to be.
You perhaps remember those silly love songs that only forty-year-olds can tolerate.

Ooo-ooo, baby. My world was empty without your love. You drive me crazy, ooo-ooo baby.

I don't care who you are or what you've done, your tender love is all I need.

You get the idea that half the world is counting on some relationship to fill their lives with contentment. But the Bible clearly states you will never be complete if you are looking anywhere other than to Jesus to meet your needs. And there's no way that you can complete someone else's life if he is missing Jesus. Therefore, take the time to prayerfully look over these guidelines. Some of these guidelines are things that you're probably already doing. If so, give yourself a pat on the back. Some of these guidelines may seem a little radical and extreme. But purity in today's culture is an extreme concept, and sometimes the only way you'll be able to guarantee success is to take extreme measures.

Tip #1: Have your parents meet the guy you wish to date before he asks you out.

Tip #2: Avoid dark solitary places when you are with a guy.

Read *Ephesians 5:11*.
Why are dark places a danger zone for dating? _____

_____

_____

_____

_____

_____

Tip #3: Develop a prayer relationship with a guy before you develop a dating relationship. If you are united together against the temptation, it's much easier than if you try to manage all the self-control by yourself. Some people are tempted and, like Jesus, they say, "Get thee behind me Satan!" A prayerless Christian might be more prone to say, "Get thee behind me Satan, and push!"

Tip #4: Just say no to "missionary dating." So what's missionary dating? A missionary date is when a Christian goes out with a non-Christian in the hopes of being a witness to the person. The courting or dating arena is not the place to begin an evangelistic emphasis.

Tip #5: Find a guy who is as committed to Jesus as you are. Answer this question: How does he view church? Is church a passionate pursuit of God for him, or is it just an excuse to see his friends? Here are a few subquestions under this category:

- Does he pray?
- Does he take notes during sermons or Bible studies?
- Does he keep a journal?
- Does he have a passion for Christian music? Praise and worship music?
- Does he volunteer to serve in ministry?
- Does he talk about how God is working around him?

If you answered yes to all these questions, you may have discovered a rare find: a righteous guy who is totally sold out to Christ. If you have no interest in dating him, at least have him put you on his prayer list. If you answered "no" to any of these questions, you better think long and hard about dating him. If you answered "no" to all these questions, this is a relationship that will be more trouble than you need. Run. Run away as fast as you can!

Tip #6: Expect to be treated like a lady. Chivalry is not dead, so make sure your date doesn't need manners CPR! Below are some general rules that you are well within your rights to expect your date to follow.

- He should open doors for you.
- He should allow you to order your meal first in a restaurant.
- He should listen and not dominate the conversation. (But be careful that you follow this same rule!)
- Ask him to pray before you eat.
- He should consult with you on your preferences and shouldn't compromise your values by taking you to places or events that compromise your reputation.

Philippians 4:8 is a good measuring stick: *Finally, brothers, whatever is true, whatever is noble, whatever is right, whatever is pure, whatever is lovely, whatever is admirable—if anything is excellent or praiseworthy—think about such things.*

Tip #7: Before your date, ask Jesus to make His presence known during your time together. Remind yourself, "I am in Christ. I don't go anywhere without Jesus. I am in His hands. I want to honor Him in all my activities and conversation."

Tip #8: Verbalize what your standards are to your date. This will ensure that there are no questions or miscommunications about expectations. Your date will also respect you for being honest and up front with him. Guys don't like to play guessing games anymore than girls do. You might try something like this:

"Josh, I'm really looking forward to our time together, but before we go out I need to talk to you about something. I've made a commitment to sexual purity, and I want to make sure that you understand how important that is to me. I'm not into having a relationship involving sexual activity or emotional manipulation. I respect you a lot, and so I wanted to be up front with you about this."

Tip #9: You are a daughter of God. Act like it! Enough said. For too long, supposedly good, Christian girls have compromised their values and integrity on the altar of sexual gratification. Some generation has got to stand up and say, "No more!"

Tip #10: Work together, act together, think together, and worship together. You don't have to go with your basic "Italian restaurant-movie-and-home-by-10:29-or-else" model for dating. As mentioned earlier, dating is really a lousy way to get to know a guy.

Tip #11: Don't be obsessed with finding God's one for you; just serve God and seek to be who God wants you to be. Then God will bring the person to you!

Tip #12: Examine your heart before you start dating. What kind of person does God want you to be? As you think about and answer this question, use the following Scripture references to guide you.

Write the Scripture reference next to the phrase that best summarizes it.
I Thessalonians 4:3; I Corinthians 6:12; I Corinthians 6:18,19; I Corinthians 8:13; I Corinthians 10:31

Don't cause others to sin   _____
Glorify God   _____
Don't be controlled   _____
Your body belongs to Christ   _____
Be holy and pure   _____

These Scriptures teach us about God's principles regarding relationships. They guide us as we determine our own personal moral standards.

Based on these scriptural principles, what kind of moral standards would you set for yourself when dating? _____
_____
_____
_____

The Good, the Bad, and....

In many cases, dating is a thoughtless, automatic act. In this context, it becomes primarily a selfish act. There are some good reasons to date; and, of course, there are also some bad reasons to date. From the reasons to date listed on the next page, check the appropriate box.

Good ❏ Bad ❏   1. Get to know someone better
Good ❏ Bad ❏   2. Prestige
Good ❏ Bad ❏   3. Spouse seeking
Good ❏ Bad ❏   4. Make someone jealous
Good ❏ Bad ❏   5. Grow socially, emotionally, spiritually
Good ❏ Bad ❏   6. Sex
Good ❏ Bad ❏   7. Fun
Good ❏ Bad ❏   8. Avoid isolation
Good ❏ Bad ❏   9. Learn how to better communicate with
                  the opposite sex
Good ❏ Bad ❏   10. Help fulfill a need to love and be loved
Good ❏ Bad ❏   11. Get a better idea of what we want our
                  future mate to look like

As you look over your markings, I think you will find that all the bad reasons to date involve reducing the other person to a means to a desired end. When trying to think of good reasons to date, try to remember the scriptural principles we studied earlier and combine them with the reasons you would like for a person to be dating you.

It's All About Attitude

Your attitude is the final factor. In *2 Corinthians 5:9*, Paul says, "We *make it our goal to please Him...*" Paul is not talking about dating in this passage. He is, however, talking about living a Christian life. Everything we do should be done to please God. That includes dating.

Do you want your dating life to please God?_____

What can you do to make sure your dating life pleases God?_____
_____
_____
_____

How can you prepare your mind? _____
_____
_____

How can you prepare your heart? _____
_____
_____

How can you plan ahead? _____
_____
_____

How can you avoid isolation?_____
_____
_____

The heart of the matter *is* your heart. Does it belong to God, to you, or to someone else? Do you desire to please God first and foremost? That is the key to maintaining a healthy and happy dating life.

Write an honest prayer to God indicating your willingness to please Him. _____
_____
_____
_____
_____
_____
_____
_____

Session 5
The Final Destination
Know Where You Are Going

So we've just about finished a cram-session on the concepts, choices, and pitfalls of courting, dating, and hanging out.

How has your view of courting, dating, and hanging out changed since you started this study? _____

_____

_____

_____

Let's wrap up by underscoring a vital truth and putting a major exclamation mark at the end of it. Begin with the final destination in mind!

Perhaps 80-90 percent of all students who are developing relationships do so without even looking at the overall purpose of this activity.

It's similar to eating Rocky Road ice cream. Why do you eat it? Is it to promote proper oral hygiene? Is it because you want to add more fiber to your diet? Is it because you want to add more muscle mass? Unless you've been brainwashed by the sales manager of a local ice cream parlor, your answer to all of the above would be no. You eat it because it tastes good and you like it.

Unfortunately most high school students develop relationships with the opposite sex, not to grow spiritually, not to develop their worldview, not to search for a lifetime mate. They do it because it feels good, it's fun, and they like it. Frankly, that answer isn't good enough in relationships. If you have that sort of approach to this whole issue, you'll wind up in situations that will be dictated by your drives and not by the standards that you set for yourself.

As one wise man once said, "Aim at nothing and you'll probably hit it." Take a few minutes now and write out a vision statement for your relationship life. _____

_____

_____

_____

_____

Take this vision statement and place it in your journal, on your calendar, on your bedroom door, or somewhere that will remind you of your purpose in developing relationships.

Relationships are all about choices. Read Hannah's choice concerning her lifestyle and dating.

My choice to take the road less traveled affects most, if not all, of my activities. Because of my convictions, I choose not to go out and get drunk and become promiscuous or do things that I know I will regret. I have found, and continue to find, new ways to have fun with my friends without compromising my beliefs. As a result of my choice, I am protected from the roads that many teenagers choose to take—the roads that lead to nothing but pain, misery, and remorse.

My choice to take the road less traveled probably affects my dating relationships the most. In my house, in order to date, we must comprise a list of standards. These standards are simply the things we are looking for in the people we will date. I did this when I was 14 years old. My standards are only shared between God, my parents, and myself. I have made a personal commitment not to compromise or ease up on these standards for anyone, at any time, under any circumstances. To some this may sound too strict and rigid, but to me it simply means I do not have to worry about dating people who I already know are not what I am looking for. In my life, I choose not to give away certain parts of my heart until God brings along the right person for me. I am not saying I will not date until I get married; I am saying I am content to wait until I find someone who is right for me at the time.

Personal Romance and Relationships True or False Test

____ There is no physical, verbal, or emotional element in my relationships that would cause me shame after I marry God's guy for me.

____ There is no element of my relationships that would cause a guy shame or ill feelings later on after he marries.

____ My heart is pure concerning words, thoughts, and actions. I want the best for the guys I date, court, or with whom I share a friendship.

____ I am not dating a guy as an attempt to fulfill my drive for self-pleasure or for approval.

____ If I were to die today, it would be true that I tried to bless him spiritually and I didn't manipulate him sexually.

____ I never gossip with the girls about the guys I date, court, or with whom I share a friendship. I speak the best of him.

God has a purpose for our relationships. The example He sets is in His relationship with us. From the creation of man in *Genesis 2* to the beginnings of the early church and even into the discussion of the end times, the primary concern of God is whether or not humanity is in relationship with Him. When God first breathed life into man's nostrils, He set up for a relationship with Himself. As part of this relationship, He blessed humanity with life and instructions for living a joyful, abundant life. Our job is to be a blessing to those around us.

Read *Leviticus 19:18.*
What does it mean to love your neighbor as yourself? ____
_____

Who is your neighbor? (See the story of the good
Samaritan for help on this one. *Luke 10:25-37)* _____
_____
_____

There are many Scriptures about blessing others. It's not a question of whether we should decide to bless others or not. It is an instruction from God.

List as many ways as you can think of to be a blessing to
others. _____
_____
_____
_____
_____

The Heart of the Matter–Loving Others as Jesus Loves Us

Take the *I Corinthians 13* **Test. Answer yes or no.**
1. **Are you patient with the growth and development of a**
   relationship? Will you have Christlike love no matter how
   much waiting you encounter? Yes
2. **Will you treat him with kindness, never mocking or**
   belittling him? Yes, intell he gave me areason not to.
3. **Will you keep pride and boasting out of your**
   relationships? No

36

4. **Will you refuse to grow bitter if a relationship ends? Are you willing to forgive and release a person if you are rejected?** NO

5. **Will you rejoice in truth?** Yes

6. **Will you not revel in things that are evil?** NO

7. **Will you protect yourself and your relationships by following God's standard?** Yes

8. **Will you give someone the same honor, blessing, and respect that God has given you?** Yes

What blessings are at the finish line for a righteous woman?

- ☑ A powerful life story
- ☐ A healthy sexual relationship with your husband
- ☐ A purpose-driven lifestyle
- ☑ A tested ability to say no when tempted
- ☑ An understanding of God's faithfulness to provide outside of your striving to provide for yourself
- ☐ A testimony of achievement
- ☐ A heritage for your children
- ☑ A blessing upon your parents and grandparents

What possibilities await a girl who didn't follow God's plan?

- ☑ Fear of Sexually Transmitted Diseases (venereal disease, AIDS, herpes)
- ☐ Inability to say no to infidelity in marriage
- ☐ Shame imputed upon you by Satan
- ☑ Feeling of dissatisfaction and regret that follows you into your marriage
- ☑ An addictive lifestyle of sex
- ☐ Emotional scars
- ☑ An inhibition to talk to your kids about abstinence and purity
- ☑ Disrespect of those closest to you

Blessed is the man who does not walk in the counsel of the wicked or stand in the way of sinners or sit in the seat of mockers. But his delight is in the law of the Lord, and on his law he meditates day and night. He is like a tree planted by streams of water, which yields its fruit in season and whose leaf does not wither. Whatever he does prospers. Not so the wicked! They are like chaff that the wind blows away. Therefore the wicked will not stand in the judgment, nor sinners in the assembly of the righteous. For the Lord watches over the way of the righteous, but the way of the wicked will perish. Psalm 1

To put this verse into the mix of what we've discussed, a righteous girl has a great future. The wicked have no future. It's as simple as that.

So where do you go from here? We challenge you to make this decision:

Lord, I accept you as Lord over my entire life. I refuse to give in to the world's view of sex and dating. I make a commitment that my life will be an example of righteous living and holy integrity. I choose to be a positive and virtuous influence on the guys rather than a temptation or a stumbling block. I choose to uplift them, not tear them down. I choose to be a transformed, active, single-minded woman who exemplifies Christian ethics in relationships. Thank you for granting me this opportunity. I want to make the most of these exciting and yet sometimes confusing years. You are all I need. I want nothing more; I will settle for nothing less.

Signed_____   **Date**_____

Leader's Guide
Easy, Practical, Fun!

Here are some tips for leading a group of students through *True Love Waits Takes a Look at Courting, Dating, and Hanging Out.*

❑ **Have extra Bibles on hand for students.** Every lesson contains a healthy dose of biblical references.

❑ **Have enough space to form two or more groups.** Sessions suggest activities involving separate girls' and guys' groups, and in some cases coed groups. Separate rooms would be preferable.

❑ **Allow your students to talk openly** about these issues in the small groups, but monitor the conversation. Try to steer them away from gutter humor or language that is inappropriate.

❑ **There are no dumb questions!** Explain to your students that this study will cover provocative issues and no one should be teased for asking a sincere question. You may even include a time for students to anonymously write questions on note cards for you to address. Students may have a question or problem that they feel uncomfortable to state out loud. This also gives you a chance to censor inappropriate questions and rephrase awkward questions.

❑ **Allow time after sessions to talk with youth** who may need some one-on-one time. Avoid opposite sex encounters. Lateral these to a leader of the same sex to avoid possible pitfalls and liabilities. There is no safe sex outside of marriage, but there can be "safe counseling" after the session.

❑ **Don't forget to prepare and have fun!** This book was never intended to be in the hands of mono-sensory, nap-inducing leaders. Make the sessions exciting, prayer-powered, and full of honest communication.

❑ **Pray everyday, for every student** that God will give them everything they need to survive the pre-honeymoon years.

Session 1

What you'll need:
☐ copies of "Qualities of Da Man!" and "Wow! Go Girl!" (p. 53)
☐ 3-minute clip from a clean, romantic movie scene
☐ TV/VCR
☐ note cards
☐ paper and pencils
☐ a copy of The Relationship Contract for each student (p. 52)

Have the students get into two groups—a guys' group and a girls' group. (You might want to divide them into subgroups if you have more than 10 in each group.) Distribute the worksheets and ask them to fill in the blanks. Girls will complete "Qualities of Da Man!" and guys will complete "Wow! Go Girl!" worksheets. Then have them share their answers with the large group and give the students time to discuss one anothers' responses. Encourage them to have fun completing the activity but also tell them to avoid crude answers. Have an adult facilitate this activity.

Show a clean, nonsexual romantic moment from an old movie. Suggestions: *Princess Bride, Casablanca, Romeo and Juliet, Sleepless in Seattle, Up Close and Personal, Ever After.* Limit the scene to two or three minutes.

Ask the group, "How is this scene like or unlike reality? Why is this considered a romantic classic?"

Ask someone in the group to read *Philippians 4:8*.

Say: "This study will require us to be accountable to each other and to be careful about the things we say and how we say them. We need to be truthful but not belittling or degrading."

Distribute The Relationship Contract to each student. Have them sign and return the contract to you.

Return students to the two small groups (guys and girls separate). Distribute note cards. Ask guys to write adjectives describing what it means to be a man and girls to write adjectives describing what it means to be a woman.

Have them stick the cards on the wall with tape.

Ask, "Apart from the obvious physical differences between men and women, what are some other things that make the two sexes distinctive?"

Ask the group, "What are the things that are most complicated about your life these days?"

Questions for the guys: "Would you say understanding girls would be on that list? Would your appetite for sex be on the list? Why or why not?"

Questions for the girls: "Would you say that understanding guys would be on the list? Would your desire for romance and companionship be on the list?"

Read *1 Corinthians 6:19* and lead in a discussion on how they can honor God with their body.

Have a student read *1 Thessalonians 4:1-5* out loud.

Ask them to discuss the following questions:
Does sex bring a person lasting satisfaction?
Can a girl alone make a guy happy and fulfilled?
Can you succeed in living a holy and pure life outside of God?

The answers of course are all "No."

Read aloud and discuss the tips for overcoming sexual temptation (p. 7 guys' book, p. 8 girls' book) and then ask the group to list any other tips that have helped them.

In conclusion ask each group to write a short letter to the group of the opposite sex using these sentence starters:
1. We know that God has called us to be pure and holy. You can help us keep our commitments to purity by...
2. We promise to help you keep your commitment by...

Return to large group and ask the groups to share their responses to the final activity with the large group.

Session 2

What you'll need:
❏ **two students ready to dramatize or read the "Laser Mouth Commercial"**
❏ **paper and pencil**

Begin the session with prayer. Ask two students to begin the session by reading a modern translation of *I Peter 5:8* and *I Corinthians 10:12-13*.

Divide the group into smaller coed groups. **Say: Make a list of products or companies which use sex and romance to sell their products.**

Ask them to create their own product and develop a short commercial to sell that product using romance.

Option: Have two students act out this **Laser Mouth Commercial:**

Guy: I was a loner, I didn't have any friends, and I certainly never got a date. In fact I used to spend my evenings eating cheese curls and organizing my sock drawer! And then...

Girl: (in a seductive tone) What you need is Acme Laser Mouth.

Guy: Wow! I had no idea my breath stunk so badly. I tried Acme Laser Mouth and now look.

Girl: (Girl walks up and puts her arms on his shoulder and smiles admiringly)

Guy: No, it's not ordinary toothpaste. It contains wintergreen plutonium which guarantees that I won't have halitosis for up to 12 nuclear hours. And now, I'm in a committed relationship with a supermodel.

Allow a few minutes, then ask them to read or perform the ads. Leaders should again make sure the ads don't cross any moral gray areas.

After this activity, gather in girls' and guys' groups again.

Tip: This session covers a huge amount of territory. Make sure you budget enough time to cover all 10 lies and cop-outs in each group.

Suggested discussion questions for the guys:

- **What are the names the Bible gives Satan? (deceiver, fallen one, accuser, liar)**
- **What do these names tell us about Satan's motives and character?**
- **What claims have you seen in magazines or TV about dating, sex, courting, and marriage that you know were lies?**
- **What are possible results of a guy who isn't mature enough to have self-control?**
- **Why do you think sex before marriage causes so much isolation in the relationship?**
- **Brainstorm ways that you can prevent being exposed to the toxic effects of pornography and sexual images. (Possible answers: finding an accountability partner, avoiding premium cable channels, avoiding channel surfing, staying away from corrupt companions, praying.)**
- **As a group, brainstorm other answers on The World's Way/ God's Way shaded chart on page 15.**
- **Where does purity end and immoral behavior begin?**

(Encourage the students to discuss healthy boundaries in dating and affection.)
• **Why do you think so many relationships end quickly after the relationship becomes sexually driven?**

Suggested discussion questions for the girls:

• **Are soap operas and secular romance novels realistic? Are they healthy to watch? Is it OK for a committed Christian girl to watch them?**
• **How can the words "I love you" be a tool of manipulation?**
• **Do you know friends who wear clothes specifically designed to attract guys? What is usually the character of a guy who is drawn in to this tactic?**
• **What are some guidelines for dressing in a God-honoring way?**
• **Where does purity end and immoral behavior begin? Encourage the students to discuss healthy boundaries in dating and affection.**
• **What can happen if you look for contentment and wholeness in a relationship with a guy?**

Bring the groups back together into the large group setting. Ask the group if they could think of any other lies or cop-outs in dating.

Pass out gray construction paper which has been cut into the shape of a bomb. See the illustration below.

Ask the students, "What are the results of all these lies and cop-outs?" Write their answers on the bombs and tape or pin them on the wall.

In conclusion, have two students read the following:
Reader #1: God says, "You are my child."
Reader #2: Satan says, "God condemns you for the sins of the past."

Reader #1: God says, "Come to me."
Reader #2: Satan says, "Hide in fear."
Reader #1: God says, "You're forgiven."
Reader #2: Satan says, "He still holds you responsible."
Reader #1: God says, "Live the life of virtue."
Reader #2: Satan says, "You'll never succeed."
Reader #1: God says, "Stand for truth."
Reader #2: Satan says, "Lies are the best shortcut."
Reader #1: God says, "Trust in me for true joy.
Reader #2: Satan says: "Don't seek God."
Reader #1: God says, "Come. Come to Me. I will meet your every need. I will guide you through the valleys of loneliness and fear. I have a plan for your life. Stay in My love, and you will not be disappointed. I will renew your strength. Wait for Me. Wait for My plan. You will mount up with wings as eagles. Trust in My power to transform you into a holy light to the world.

Close in prayer.

Session 3

What you'll need:
- ❑ **two or more adults prepared to tell a story**
- ❑ **note cards**
- ❑ **several poster boards in the shapes of street signs**
- ❑ **ice cream and toppings**
- ❑ **bowls and spoons**

Ask a student to read *Psalm 37:3-7*. Introduce them to this session by discussing how important it is to use this Scripture as a guideline for choosing relationship lifestyles. Pray with the group, asking God to give them patience and wisdom.

Give each student a card. Ask them to write a definition of dating.

Have one of the adult leaders tell a story of her favorite dating memory. Have another adult tell about an embarrassing moment he had during a date.

After the two stories, ask some students to volunteer to read their definition of dating.

Mock Minidebate
Tell the students you are going to have a mock minidebate on the merits of courting, dating, and hanging out. A few days before this meeting you will need to select one adult to represent dating, another to represent courting, and another to represent hanging out. You will need a moderator who will make sure that each side is heard.

After the debate, ask the students to vote for their preference by secret ballot. Calculate the votes and share the results. Facilitate a discussion on these three approaches.

Divide the large group into coed small groups and ask students to develop their own traffic signs that would be unique warnings for courting, dating, and hanging out.

Dating signs examples:
Danger! Steep Commitment Ahead
Darkness! Beware of Falling Temptation

Courting signs examples:
Be Alert! Accelerated Seriousness Possible

Allow the groups to display their signs and talk about them.

Separate the guys and the girls into learning rooms or areas and work through the Start-up lists on page 22 of the girls' book and page 25 of the guys' book.

Complete the session 15 minutes early if possible. **Say: We've had a pretty detailed discussion about the pro's and the con's of dating** and courting, and we've spent a little time on the concept of hanging out. So we wanted to surprise you with a 15-minute self-demonstration of hanging out.

Surprise them with an ice cream party.

After giving them some time to eat and hang out, close the session in prayer. Pray that we all make the choices that God wants us to make. Pray that within the relationships that the students have with the opposite sex, they will place Jesus as the foundation of it all.

Session 4

What you'll need:
❑ **students or adults to help read or dramatize scenes**
❑ **large mural paper**
❑ **candy, cheap prize, or blue ribbon**
❑ **poster or PowerPoint slide of the relationship diagram**

Begin the session by having two students help you set up the idea of pitfalls that we encounter in relationships.

The Pressure Pitfall
Male: I just don't understand why. There's no reason for you to be afraid. I'm not going to hurt you. I'm frustrated. I need you. Why don't you just give in? I love you. What's wrong with it? If you truly love a person you should have the freedom to express it.
Female: I was just hoping that...
Male: Hoping for what? Hoping that I would just stick around and wait for you to make up your mind about whether you love me or not?
Female: It's not a matter of love.
Male: You don't even know what love is about! The only thing you care about is yourself. What about me? What about my needs?

The Boredom Pitfall

Male: So what do you want to do?

Female: I don't care. Whatever you want to do.

Male: Doesn't matter to me.

Female: We could go out.

Male: Yeah, we could.

Female: Whatever, sweetie.

Male: I don't care.

Female: I guess we could just stay here on the couch.

Male: Good idea. I bet we can think of something.

The In-Love Stupor Pitfall

(They look into each other's eyes and lovingly say...)

Female: John

Male: Marsha

Female: John

Male: Marsha

Female: John

Male: Marsha

Ask the students if they can think of any other pitfalls. After some discussion, invite the students to gather in several groups and create separate graffiti walls. Invite them to write on the walls some of their favorite cornball love song lyrics and any (tasteful) illustrations they can draw.

After a few minutes, let them share their graffiti walls with the whole group and challenge them to sing a few lines. Encourage them to have fun. Give a blue ribbon and some candy to the winning team.

After this activity, divide the group into same-gender groups for the second half of the session.

Talk through the 12 tips. (p. 27 of the girls' book, p. 30 of the guys' book)

When you get to the "missionary dating" segment, read the following story aloud:

A Divine Revelation for Danny

I'd been a Christian about five years when I met Angela who was in several of my classes. We became friends. She was absolutely the most incredibly good-looking girl I'd ever gotten to know as a friend. After a while, I knew that if I asked her out she'd say yes. But I also knew she didn't have the same kind of relationship with Christ that I did. I tried to rationalize it by saying that her family goes to mass and so she must have a relationship, somehow, with Jesus. But the topic rarely came up about spirituality. So I decided on my own that I'd date her in order to try and lead her to Christ. Big mistake. As we became more intimate I felt guilty, and the guilt made me become less open to talking about my faith because I didn't want to appear to be a hypocrite.

One night I had a dream that I was preparing for the youth mission trip that summer. We were loading the buses full of supplies and equipment before we left. Angela came by to see me; and before I knew it we were alone, and we began to kiss on the bus! A few seconds later in the dream, Rick, my youth minister, stepped onto the bus and asked if he could talk with me. I was humiliated. He asked me if this was a good idea—me kissing Angela on the bus the night before we left on the mission trip. In the dream, I just shrugged my shoulders and said, "Sure, Rick, I'm actually witnessing to her."

After I thankfully woke up from this crazy dream, I realized how stupid it was for me to think that I could win Angela to Christ by dating her.

Say: Danny did a good job of expressing on paper the absurdity of the idea that dating can be a great place to win girls to Christ. Here's a surefire rule of thumb. Date Christians. Pray for non-Christians.

Explain the following illustration to the students.

Concept: A couple in a dating or courting relationship needs to realize the importance of spiritual growth as individuals. If they are seeking to know God in all His fullness, they will be more capable of establishing real respect and closeness to and for each other. If one is growing spiritually and the other is moving away, the closeness can never be achieved.

49

Read aloud the Scriptures found on p. 30 of the girls' book and p. 33 of the guys' book. *I Thessalonians 4:3; I Corinthians 6:12; I Corinthians 6:18, 19; I Corinthians 8:13; I Corinthians 10:31.*

Ask students to pray about whether they are willing to live by God's principles. Remind them that not following the plan and guidelines He set forth can be spiritually deadening to any relationship. Allow them to spend some time praying. Allow students to pair up with a member of the opposite sex and take turns praying for each other's commitments. Tell them they should leave quietly after they review the material and pray about the commitments they are making.

Session 5

What you'll need:
❏ **pastor, youth minister, or Christian counselor for Q&A time**
❏ **stones (enough for every group member to have one)**
❏ **worship music**
❏ **envelopes and note cards with a "result" (listed below)**
Results: Herpes; AIDS; An unwanted pregnancy; Feelings of shame; Lack of trust; Emotional depression and abuse; Problems in your future marriage; Legal action against you

Gather the students and have a student that you've contacted earlier read his vision statement for his relationship life. (Make sure you set this up ahead of time. Don't pick the person on the spur of the moment.) Begin this final session with prayer. As you wrap up the study, lead the students into an anonymous Q&A where they can write questions about courting, dating, and hanging out on note cards. You might want the pastor or youth minister to be the moderator.

After this go directly into gender groups. If your group hasn't written their vision statement for their relationship life, then allow them to do so and ask for volunteers to share them with the group.

Read the following rendering of *2 Corinthians 4:1-4*.

Since through God's bold and unbelievable mercy we have this God-controlled mission, we don't resort to gutter mentality. But instead we say farewell to slave-driven, shame-induced meandering. We don't have any reason to tweak the gospel or distort the message. It's just the opposite. We can let the message run wild, and it will find its way into the hearts of people. And if they can't see it, it is because they can't get off the treadmill of death. The one who runs the show down here, the liar, has blindfolded their cranium, and they can't see the glory of Christ, who is God. (paraphrased)

Say: Vision statements are important because they give us a foundation for our actions.

In the small groups, discuss the Personal Romance and Relationships True or False Test. Ask them if they have any other good additions to the test.

Return to the large group.

The Envelopes
Explain that when you lose your standards and/or purity in relationships, you are risking your future. Give each student an envelope with a card inside. **Say: Imagine you have allowed yourself to break God's standards. When you do this many times the results are invisible at first, but they do appear.** Ask each student to read what his or her card says.

In Search of a Dream Team
Give each student a rock. Explain to them that in the Old Testament, God's people at significant moments in history took rock to build an altar as a sign of their commitment to and worship of God. Underscore how important it is to remain pure as they seek the ultimate destination of a holy life.

Play worship music. Suggested Songs: "Holiness" (Sonic Flood, Gotee Records 1999); "Step by Step" by Rich Mullins (Songs 2, Reunion Records, 1999); "Spirit of the Living God," No. 244, *The Baptist Hymnal*, 1991; music from "WOW Worship 2000" (Integrity Music, Marathana! Music, and Vineyard Music, 2000). Ask the students to block out all distractions and pray for wisdom in deciding what relationship choices they need to make. Suggest that they confess any past actions that were contrary to God's plan. Invite students who are willing to surrender all their relationships to God's plan to bring their stone to the center of the room and kneel in prayer. Close after a few minutes with an audible prayer of thanksgiving.

Conclude by allowing the students to share how this study has affected them. Allow them the opportunity to share new insights and discoveries. Close by challenging them to find an accountability partner if they don't have one yet and continue to work together to make sure their relationships in courting, dating, and hanging out are pure before God.

The Relationship Contract

As a student of God's Word and a seeker of truth, I covenant with God and this group that I will:

Speak truthfully, but without an intent to harm any individual in the group. I will be open to hear what God has to say about courting, dating, and hanging out. If someone in the group shares personal information in the small group, I promise to keep confidence and not share things without permission of the person.

Signed _____   Date _____

Qualities of Da Man!

(To be completed by the girls.)

A lot of guys think that we are attracted to them because of _____
_____. But the truth is that we care more about _____
_ _____.

Guys sometimes don't _____, which really makes us feel
_____. Sometimes guys don't know how to control their
_____. The qualities of a great guy include _____,
_____, _____, _____,
and _____.

The qualities of a nightmare date include _____, _____,
_____, and _____.

Wow! Go Girl!

(To be completed by the guys.)

A lot of girls think that we are attracted to them because of _____
_____. But the truth is that we care more about _____
_ _____.

Girls sometimes don't _____, which really makes us feel
_____. Sometimes girls don't know how to control their
_____. The qualities of a great girl include _____,
_____, _____, _____,
and _____.

The qualities of a nightmare date include _____, _____,
_____, and _____.

Two Ways to Earn Credit
for Studying LifeWay Christian Resources Material

CONTACT INFORMATION:
Christian Growth Study Plan
One LifeWay Plaza, MSN 117
Nashville, TN 37234
CGSP info line 1-800-968-5519
www.lifeway.com/CGSP
To order resources 1-800-485-2772

Christian Growth Study Plan resources are available for course credit for personal growth and church leadership training.

Courses are designed as plans for personal spiritual growth and for training current and future church leaders. To receive credit, complete the book, material, or activity. Respond to the learning activities or attend group sessions, when applicable, and show your work to your pastor, staff member, or church leader. Then go to *www.lifeway.com/CGSP*, or call the toll-free number for instructions for receiving credit and your certificate of completion.

For information about studies in the Christian Growth Study Plan, refer to the current catalog online at the CGSP Web address. This program and certificate are free LifeWay services to you.

Need a CEU?

CONTACT INFORMATION:
CEU Coordinator
One LifeWay Plaza, MSN 150
Nashville, TN 37234
Info line 1-800-968-5519
www.lifeway.com/CEU

Receive Continuing Education Units (CEUs) when you complete group Bible studies by your favorite LifeWay authors.

Some studies are approved by the Association of Christian Schools International (ACSI) for CEU credits. Do you need to renew your Christian school teaching certificate? Gather a group of teachers or neighbors and complete one of the approved studies. Then go to *www.lifeway.com/CEU* to submit a request form or to find a list of ACSI-approved LifeWay studies and conferences. Book studies must be completed in a group setting. Online courses approved for ACSI credit are also noted on the course list. The administrative cost of each CEU certificate is only $10 per course.